Traces And Blossoms

Nada Menzalji

Translated by Atef Alshaer

I would like to thank the poet Monzer Masri, who was behind the publication of my first poem, for his continuous support.

And I would like to thank the poet Maram Al Masri, who translated my poems into French and introduced me to the French cultural milieu.

I also would like to thank Dr Jennifer Langer and Dr David Clark for their great support.

To my husband Soran Maroof, who with love accommodates my mood swings and listens to my draft poems.

To my eldest brother Abdel Majid, who taught me to question and doubt, and to understand beauty at its deepest

To my brother, the short story writer, Maher, who gave me the first book in my life.

To my dearest friend Enas Najjari, who makes me feel that I am a great poet.

Above all, I am grateful to my novelist and translator mother Nadia Chouman. I am that small branch from her tree. She gave me all that I need to become a writer.

"Perhaps some day I'll crawl back home, beaten, defeated. But not as long as I can make stories out of my heartbreak, beauty out of sorrow."

Sylvia Plath

CONTENTS

From "Thefts Of A Nameless Poet"
*** From "Thefts Of A Nameless Poet" and published In French in "Anthologie Femme Poetes Du Mond Arab"*

Healing

The house takes you for all its people
it awaits you
resting its cheek on its arm
the house falls asleep
the cat waits for you
it thinks you are a wool ball, preserving its hunter's instinct
threads of dust think you are sunlight
evening thinks you the air, hanging its black shirt
scent runs towards you, thinking you are a bee,
securing its eternity
the bed, it makes me laugh!
the bed shrinks, ashamed of its scandalous longing for you
as for me, I am healed of deluded thought
I am not waiting for you,
I know I am not waiting for you
I leave darkness to stretch as if nothing else will happen.

More Than One Resemblance

I look like the land
but the land bears fruit
and I am barren
it embraces me, while people abandon me
it remains but I fade away.

I look like the road
it never ends
while I remain standing in my place.

I look like the wind
it runs wildly in the prairies
while my hair wraps on me

I look like a mountain
steadfast in its place
while I am shaken by a passing breeze

I look like the house
secure and safe
while I am shame
revealed by a lonely tear.

I look like a candle
it lights up
while I am darkness
which cannot melt away.

I look like my mother
she has her kindness
while I am a prisoner of my needs.
I look like a cigarette
an enjoyment for moments
and burning forever.

I am half flesh
and half diamond.
I look like birds
but
there are no wings to carry me away
my arms always break
and I fall
to the ground

Naked Life

There comes a time when you no longer care for your secrets
It is no secret that you do not have any secrets
like other women with naked life
you continue to sweep the floor
and empty the wardrobes of their contents
Your obsession is polishing the mirror
even though spirits no longer appear
the moment you shut the door
the spirits you secretly treasured
cleaners threw them out with their fat gloves

You open the windows widely
the air comes in
and goes out lightly just as it came
the air, weightless, without secrets
without trace
to be swept away.

Always Late On Love

love might reach my heart
while I am late
as always happens to me with important encounters
at the last moment I search for the house key
I find only the lock.

I return to the kitchen and
the glass falls from my hand
it shatters
my hand bleeds as I collect it
that is how love wounds me
before we even meet!

A Red Star

Neither man is her man
nor is she his woman
and here they are like a bed and its cover
attached
heavy
silent in their wet secret.

His hands are in her hair
his heart is on her heart
her lips are slightly pursed
as if she was murmuring something in his ear
she lets out a deafening cry
one word could have summed up life.

His face is immersed in the lushness of her neck
she cannot push away the stranger
he cannot breathe in the breeze from her perfume
between them, a light broke down.

He threw himself on her
she did not cry
she did not call for rescue
she did not push him away
from her riverbanks
there was slight trembling
she opened up her arms
as if she was going to embrace him
then she left them open

two neutral doves
lying on both sides of her
a whole world came into being
from the first and last embrace.

He was going to say something
but forgot it
he was about to be confused
but he forgot the confusion.

*

Calmness
as if in the depth of a cocoon
they laid one cover on them
they carried them together
and the camera recorded
one moment after another
a red star
growing
blossoming
running down in one long stream
from here
to where the gods sleep.

*

Here I am clinging to the trunk of a palm tree
I have just caught my dream
as he caught me
freedom...

Virtual Safety

The thin smoke
paints a cloud over the mirror
there is no rain today
as there was no rain yesterday
there is no blossom in the earth's womb
to tempt the bee
and silence does not fit prayer

A fly has just ended
its surveillance mission
around the globe
a spherical model of planet earth.

*

Beyond the virtual seas
there are virtual young men
absorbed by a game
as if they have discovered it just now
it has simple rules
bare chests
the military
and bullets
the military fires bullets
and the young men compete to fall down
their wings flap towards the sky
without interrupting their long scream
Freedom!

Young men with two dimensions or three

red roses on an asphalt of virtual roads.

*

loudspeakers announce:
"we promise you a smooth transition
from a human sperm
to a fit sheep"
a sheep reassured by barking dogs in the pastures
so it chews more grass
it could grant
with such good intention
its flesh, wraps of shawarma
with pickles.

*

But the cat that ate its offspring
practices innocence
and chases a virtual mouse
and the virtual young men
with provocative bare chests
they are prisoners in your screen.
As for your good husband
he is there on the hilltop
playing the flute
and sperms dance to his tunes.

*

Rest your body stuffed with boredom
rest your fear
and sleep
sleep on the riverbank, where myths sing of
your running river in a bath

disinfected with Dettol
suffocated with cement
as words revolve around it,
upside down on their back
sleep
sleep
until tomorrow
or after, after tomorrow
or after, after, after tomorrow
freedom, the nightmare
the game of the virtual young men won't disturb your sleep
for the first condition of freedom and not its last
does not come except
for those who day and night
respond to its urgent call.

The Charm Of Angels

All the angels I knew
loved me
their heavenly duties burdened them
I pardoned them
they left their little wounds with me
bleeding in the night
and left rough feathers
not even enough
to fill a pillow.

Every prince I kissed
reverted to being a frog.
I am waiting
though much time has passed
for a devil
who has lost his way.

Where Can I Find Something Like Love

Indifference in love, most cruel,
at the peak of its intensity, it gives up on you
where can I find something like love...

*

Love
Not as it was written about by little gold-diggers
who make curtains out of kisses
and beds out of hugs
but as it is known by the sons of temptation
for they do not know how to halt their excess
you know them from their laughter
the passionate
the deceitful
it has the voice of sparrows' chirping
at their first taste of freedom

In the excess of love
they break their hearts
and stand with their hands tied
enchanted
– lords of love –
then they ignite the fire in what remains

At the peak of its intensity, it abandons you
and its dearth kills
where can I find something like love?

Loneliness

O loneliness,
great
like a goddess
I am your prisoner
your desiring slave
your cave's entrance
an atom in your ashes
plaster on your hand's wound

Do not leave me
like a latch in a derelict house
like a broken plate
like supper, left over from the night before

O loneliness
do not leave me
among others
alone!

Alice

She came from the country of the Tsunami
she carries keys to houses she does not live in
she cooks delicious food but is reduced to a boiled egg
she irons clothes and hopes to put them on after they wear down
she speaks to the vicar in an unrecognisable language
he becomes confused with his Christ
it was said the English police caught her red handed
as she was sweeping others' dust
it was said a gang was asking her to pay hush money
it was said she had an indecent secret job
without a passport or any personal documents
Alice disappeared
not even one lover asked after her.

*

Alice did not clean her sheets
the remains of her oily hair sat in the sink
she left the marks of their shoes on the stairs
as in the chase game
a scandalous light beam seeped through the curtains' split
and the heartless men who dragged her
filled the air with their odour
and the air disappeared under the rug.

In the attic, where Alice was living
there are pressed sorrows like a clove of garlic
the body which has just emerged out of a well
is drowning in sticky fog.

Her tears stream down her cheeks
they leave behind a long trail
the tears of the woman
who indulges in tasting hot chillies
and drinks her pleasure from the bottle.

Her breasts are two big balloons
they jerked up slightly
the air arrested her at a moment of liberation
her sky is low
or even lower
her voice shot up
travelling higher and higher to the sky
enchanting
the free one dies, but she won't sacrifice her breasts
she stumbled upon the ceiling of the room
she fell down with teeth marks on her left breast.

*

Alice is lying down
next to a pair of shoes
all her belongings are tucked away in a black plastic bag
she dreams she went into her hat
she grew like a brown mushroom
she sank like a teardrop
absorbed by the pavement...

Cinema

When we died
we did not give the matter much thought
we were assured of the inevitable happy ending
to the old Hollywood film
the sort that never leaves an audience in tears
we thought why not sleep a little?
Let us be awakened by the director
We shall return from the land of sleep
to a delightful ending
and we wait and we wait for it
in vain do we wait for the joyful scene
like chrysanthemums scorched by the sun
we too fade away.

A little girl with two dark plaits and a red coat
lives her first adventure in the cinema
the little girl of long ago
reaches up for her mother's hands
engulfed in darkness with a long tail.

The audience were dead
and the film did not end
the heroes were dead
and the film did not end
the little girl was dead
and the film did not end
the coat was dirty and in tatters
and the coat was dead.

The hero will marry the heroine behind the screen
just as in the poster
from the once beautiful era
if only the romantic female lead of the story
had not died
the film had not reached its close
the lover-hero who so much longed to conclude the movie
with a kiss
died.

Who guides the souls to their abodes?
or are they swept away by winds?

Two dead braids...
The movie did not end
the movie died.

Light Farewell

How beautiful to say goodbye
lightly
my hands in my pockets
holding the cold.
I blew it away
"goodbye"
an ambiguous smile
one light word
a falling cloud.
I am tempted by farewell
one like a falling leaf from its own tree
I let the sparrow flee from my own bosom
and slowly I turn around
like someone sending a kiss into the air
a rose
with softness to bloody the cheek.

With withdrawal that provokes no one's doubt
I leave the stage
after my marginal appearance.

How beautiful to say goodbye
without waiting till the last scene
believing in some way that
I am leaving
but I am not dying,
or am I dying?

Trustworthy

Blind
I forget to dye my grey hair for him
trustworthy
I lend him my back in the bath
companionable
I leave the door open for him
miaows between my legs
he is my cover when I am cold
intimate
I exchange my underwear with him
chaste
like a pregnant woman in her last trimester
he goes missing
I do not think I am alone in his absence
that is
old love.

Absence

In my absence
fat doves will come down
maybe an ant will have a date with its friend-ant in my
     windowsill
maybe the snail, that letter scriber, has passed by
and left me one of its ambiguous letters
maybe a bee desired to change the scent of flowers
maybe butterflies were forced to flee collectively
or maybe a flock of sparrows
maybe spiderwebs built their emirate
and an infiltrator came and destroyed it.

Maybe cloves blossomed before the dahlia
maybe the gardenia was made infertile this summer
maybe the grass invaded the land of memories

Maybe all of this will take place in my absence
leaving only doubt behind

Their traces
and my traces
when we become equal
in absence.

Beyond Hope

Some time ago I found hope
sitting in a wardrobe
stacked with ideas for years
forgotten
some of them became tight
and others more loose than appropriate
change is constant
as befits the size of my aspirations
hope was elusive
akin to impossible
I trimmed its sleeves
I enlarged its armhole
I changed the location of buttons
I lengthened it on one side
and shortened it on another
when I finished amending it
its impossibility grew complete.

Happiness

I have spent my life waiting for it
at arrival, it emptied its bowels on me
it seems happiness never recognised me
it thought that I am a tree
it seems I did not recognise it
I thought it was a dog!

Deficiency

In the kingdom of deficiency
there is no complete homesickness
or belonging
or love to satisfy the heart
or hatred to overwhelm it
there is't a narrow prison
or a wide space
or living to excite the minds
or a suitable death.

*

The secret
the secret, I say to you
is in the abandonment
when you are free
you grow more
and the more you grow
the more you are free
you arrive
and the more you arrive
the more you grow full
it is the soul
leave it to its own path
and live for yourself
you who will vanish.

Then We Do Not Weep

It fell on us to witness
how the buffalos peed by the river-head
and we had to drink
engulfed by such sadness
and we were not supposed to weep
for tears are such an inadequate surmise.

*

We will continue on our path
as clowns
we meet people with our real faces
but they laugh

*

The defeat comes naked
but they say: it is summer
and the swimmer tempts the sea.

Turtle

Turtle
and I am not concerned to compete
with any hare
I carry my heart on my back
a house
and slip into the depth of love.

Silence

For a long time
I have no longer told anyone
what is happening with me

When I pass by a tree
I turn my head
and whistle a merry tune
trees like mothers
their sorrow is painful
I prefer the company of pebbles
their hearts are hard
and everyone tramples on them.

Shawl Of Lace

O woman
you are mistaken when you think
loneliness is not a shawl of lace
you remove it from your shoulder
when you desire a kiss from the sun
love stings the lonely heart
without it knowing.

The Choice Of Jasmine

Why does a jasmine flower
choose me
as the only witness for its suicide?
I am so concerned to leave,
with more than what birth
had bestowed upon me
I do not need anyone to remind me
life's thread is drawn from the needle hole
of our life with the same silence
but without the same tenderness.

Ageing

Welcome the wrinkles
welcome the kind sloppiness
welcome the nose that grows bigger with time
welcome the hair, the witness of age
welcome the parched lips that do not deny kisses
welcome the waist burrowed in loose flesh
welcome beauty tiptoeing away
welcome as you fade slowly
like a silken dress beyond all repair.

Dark Spots

I know Maida Vale
indeed, I know it
I pronounce its name lightly now
as a blind woman might know the history of places by intuition
the smells' whisperer
the parameter of colours.

*

The footsteps in the road
the hand trembling in the keyhole
Maida Vale!
A bridge to love's bank
everything was ready
I even lit candles.

A big house in Maida Vale
It must have been owned by somebody
before it was claimed by my memory.

I am a butterfly, buzzing around his lips
I am a wool ball
its threads untied by his fingers
in his presence, my jaws hurt
but I cannot stop smiling!

I am the woman
who sneaked to others' houses
in others' cities
to wait her man

she wouldn't lose him
with all his different names.

The usually decent trees in the street
quickly striped off,
my lover
passed by.

*

The window cleaner comes
and goes...
he has been coming and going for years
he climbs the ladder to the window of the highest floor
this is my bedroom.

I am ready to let him enjoy spying on an empty room
If only I did not look so much like those lonely women
turning between sheets
in my silken night gown with one cut strap

I sabotaged the past
with longing, so attached to me,
like siamese twins
with two heads
but only one bra.

Had the window cleaner not taken me by surprise
this time also
preoccupied
totally with the lighting of candles.

*

Yes, I know Maida Vale
I 'play topsy-turvy' with cities
put the names of streets in the blender
add houses like ice cubes
let them turn, making an infernal noise
crushing memory
I light up my cigarette
I scrutinise the dark spots
marking the back of my hands
I am getting older
I have such desire
for talking
and as an unacceptable compensation
I grow more skilled
at concealment.